ONE OF
AMERICA'S
FAVORITES

INDEPENDENT AMERICAN
FOOD PRODUCTS SURVEY

NEW YORK

AMERICA'S FAVORITES

Edited by Kay & Marshall Lee

G. P. PUTNAM'S SONS

Library of Congress Cataloging in Publication data
Main entry under title:

Lee, Kay.
    America's favorites.
    1. Food habits—United States.   2. Food preferences—United States.
3. Food industry and trade—United States.   I. Lee, Marshall, 1921-
joint author.   II. Title. GT2853.U5L43   641'.01'3   80-16650
ISBN *0-399-12514-0*

ACKNOWLEDGMENTS: Our thanks to Patricia Finneran for her help in preparing the content of this book, to Myron Miller who made some of the photographs, and to the many people in the American food, confection, and beverage industries who cooperated in our effort to achieve the highest standards of quality and accuracy.

EDITOR'S NOTE

The inclusion of any product in this book should not be taken as an endorsement of that product by the Independent American Food Products Survey, the editors, or the publisher; nor an endorsement by the manufacturer of that product or any other product included in the book; nor an endorsement of this publication, any person or company associated with it, or the IAFPS by the manufacturer of the product. The selection of the products included was made by the editors on the basis of information provided by the IAFPS, but no relationship exists between the latter and any person or company associated with the manufacture or marketing of the products included.

Foreword

America's Favorites is a time capsule for the 25th Century. It presents in formal array 75 of the most popular and enduring foods, confections, and beverages of America in our time.

Each one of America's favorites is as familiar and beloved as the Statue of Liberty, Whistler's Mother, a Norman Rockwell cover, or a Grandma Moses landscape—and is as much a part of America's heritage. Although intended only for direct passage from maker to consumer, most of these products are among the most advertised objects in America, so they are visual icons of our culture as well as favorite comestibles. When historians of the future view (what may be left of) American life in this century, they will find in *America's Favorites* 75 of its most pervasive and significant images. It is fitting that these images should be recorded with the same high standard of reproduction and documentation as works of art and other classic artifacts. This we have tried to do.

A fairly small number of the products have appeared during the recent past and zoomed to the top of the heap, but most of them are old favorites, dating back to the childhood of even the most senior readers. Names like Cracker Jack and Wheaties are as nostalgic as they are familiar. It is tempting to look for some common factor in the extraordinary popularity of these 75 products. Perhaps it is that they are almost all quick, easy antidotes for the frustrations of our daily lives.

Each country has dishes and treats that give pleasure, comfort, and lift in time of need. A nice cup of hot tea will soothe the most harried Britisher; a plate of pasta will make any Italian purr anytime; for the Germans, things go best with a wurst, or a whipped-cream-smothered torte. In America, abundance has produced a whole constellation of things to eat and drink for sure gratification and instant solace. The favorites among them not only taste good, but seem to make life smoother. Many are "momma food", soft and warm, easy to chew, often sweet. Others seem designed to cheer—a little tingly on the tongue, sometimes salted, often crackly, or spicy, or icy. Always they are convenient to find and use. (A 1980

U.S. Government survey found that half of the foods consumed in American homes are convenience foods.)

Curiously, beverage favorites are drunk ice-cold—often with hot food—or piping hot. Merely cool or room-temperature drinks like the wines, beers, and waters of Europe are making some inroads in the United States, but mostly they get a dose of ice cubes to make them right. The flip side of America's love of oral comfort seems to be a passion for stimulating contrasts.

Note how many of the favorites have names with either the warm roundness of a momma's hug—Oreo, Milky Way, Eggo, Sno Balls, Marshmallow Fluff—or bright, happy, cheery sounds—Twinkies, 7UP, Snickers, Fritos, and of course, Kisses. Can it be doubted that the makers of these treats understand their appeal to folks in need of comfort and cheer?

Many of the food favorites in these pages are consumed at mealtimes, but most are, or can be, used as snacks to satisfy moments of desire. The occasion might be an off-time pang of hunger or thirst, an empty hour to fill, or a sudden need to lighten the stress of living and working. To a considerable extent, these goodies go with festive times, and many are as traditional as the occasions themselves.

Who are the consumers of America's favorites? Children of all ages gobble up a large part of the confection and soft drink selection. Sports spectators and movie watchers (including TV watchers) account for cosmic quantities of hot dogs, hamburgers, popcorn, TV dinners and, again, soft drinks. Families with hard-working parents eat often of convenience foods—open-and-eat or mix-with-water-heat-and-eat. With some regularity they visit fast food establishments where no preparation effort at all is needed. Packaged baked goods are downed by the millions during coffee breaks in shops and offices all over America. Even the most con-firmed devotee of natural foods secretly gulps a forbidden favorite when the temptation gets too strong. (Ask one sometime—they usually confess.) The answer to our question then is: Probably *everyone*.

The 75 selections in this book are based on a study conducted by the Independent American Food Products Survey. The available statistics were consulted, but there are too many variables—dura-tion on the market, regional factors, advertising budgets, distribu-tion facilities—to justify a choice by sales figures alone.

Even if all the sales figures were compiled and weighted

for the variables, in most cases they would not be significant because many of the products selected are unique and their popularity cannot be directly measured against any other one. Most of those that do fall into a general category are different enough from their competitors so that a consumer does not necessarily choose one, but may buy two or more brands of that group. In some cases, one product is clearly the biggest seller of its kind, and this fact usually—but not always—coincides with popular feeling. In other cases, the product itself is so widely enjoyed that no single brand represents it—take brownies, cream cheese, macaroni and cheese, etc.

Taken into account is the impact a product has made on the popular consciousness: Cracker Jacks, peanuts, and animal crackers have been enshrined in song—the latter is even the title of a movie and "Peanuts" is the title of a most popular comic strip; Campbell's Tomato Soup and Coca-Cola have been the subjects of famous works of art; names like Spam, Wheaties, Twinkies, and Tootsie Roll are household words, well known even to those who may never have tasted the products. No sales or market-share figures could push these favorites off the list. Finally, there is the element of affection—an intangible that lies at the heart of the selection and cannot be measured, only sensed. In the end, the choice has to be made on the basis of historical and personal factors as much as statistics.

Certainly, some will say that other products should have been included. Each of us has our own personal favorites and some of these might very well qualify for selection, but if these 75 foods, confections, and beverages are not the *only* favorites, together they present a valid picture of what we prefer, and as such are well entitled to be called America's Favorites.

K & M L

Campbell's Tomato Soup

DIMENSIONS: 10¾ oz. can: 4″ H × 2⅝″ Diam.

PACKAGE: Steel can with ¼ lb. tin coating. Paper label printed four-color offset lithography.

ORIGINATOR: John T. Dorrance

DATE OF ORIGIN: late 19th Century

INGREDIENTS: Water, tomato paste, corn syrup, wheat flour, salt, partially hydrogenated vegetable oils (soybean oil, palm or cottonseed oil), natural flavoring, ascorbic acid (vitamin C), citric acid.

MAKER: Campbell Soup Company, Camden, New Jersey

SLOGAN: "M'm! M'm! Good!"

TRADEMARK: The Campbell Kids

NOTES: Joseph Campbell and Abram Anderson began a partnership in 1869 to can tomatoes, vegetables, jellies, condiments, and mincemeat. Arthur Dorrance replaced Anderson in 1891. Although the company was then named the Joseph Campbell Preserve Company, it was J. T. Dorrance, Arthur's nephew, who in 1897 originated the concept of canned condensed soup. The red-and-white label was suggested by the colors of Cornell College. The Campbell Kids were created by artist Grace Gebbie in 1904. In the 1960s, the Campbell's Tomato Soup can was immortalized by artist Andy Warhol as a symbol of America.

    The Joseph Campbell Preserve Company began advertising in New York City's streetcars in 1899, and this practice was an important part of the efforts to launch Campbell's Tomato Soup.

Campbell's is a trademark of Campbell Soup Company.

Fritos® BRAND Corn Chips

DIMENSIONS: 12″ H × 7½″ W × 3½″ D

PACKAGE: Polyethylene, polypropylene plastic bag, printed by flexography. Label designed by Brooks-Bradley Printing Company, San Antonio, Texas.

ORIGINATOR: Elmer Doolin

DATE OF ORIGIN: 1932

INGREDIENTS: Corn, vegetable oil (contains one or more of the following: corn oil, peanut oil, soybean oil or sunflower oil), salt.

MAKER: Frito-Lay, Inc., Dallas, Texas

SLOGANS: "Truly Krisp and Tender"; "Tastes Better with Fritos® Corn Chips"; "Buy Two and Hide One For You"; "Munch, Munch, Munch a Bunch of Fritos® Corn Chips"; "Muncha Bunch®"; "I'll Munch To That®"

NOTES: Young Texan Elmer Doolin purchased the recipe (based on the traditional Mexican tortilla, a small flat cake of pounded cornmeal), the equipment, and 19 local accounts from a Mexican for $100. Doolin and his mother made the chips in Mrs. Doolin's kitchen. He then put the bagged chips into display racks that he had built himself and persuaded reluctant merchants to use them in place of the old-fashioned glass jars. The rest is food history.

Hires® Root Beer

DIMENSIONS: 16 oz. bottle: 11⅛" H × 2³⁸⁄₆₄" Diam.

PACKAGE: Glass with metal cap. Design by Tom Cain and Associates

ORIGINATOR: Charles E. Hires, Sr.

DATE OF ORIGIN: 1876

INGREDIENTS: Carbonated water, nutrative sweetener (sugar or corn sweetener), caramel color, phosphoric acid, natural and artificial flavor, preserved with ¹⁄₁₀% sodium benzoate.

MAKER: Hires Division, Crush International Inc., Evanston, Illinois

SLOGANS: "Hires to You!"; "Catch a Draft".

NOTES: Pharamacist C. E. Hires was served an herb tea during his honeymoon in New Jersey. He enjoyed the flavor so much that upon returning to his drugstore in Philadelphia, he created a drink from root, bark, and berries, which he named Hires Herb Tea. A friend, then the president of Columbia University, suggested the name be made congenial to the beer-drinking habits of the Philadelphia public, so the product was renamed Hires Root Beer. A merchandising genius, Hires gave out free samples, took newspaper ads, and created trade cards with a color picture on one side and an ad on the other. The cards were given free to customers, who began to collect them much as baseball cards were collected later. Sales soared.

Hires® is a registered trademark of Crush International Inc., Evanston, Illinois.

Macaroni and Cheese

ORIGINATORS: Probably the Etruscans

DATE OF ORIGIN: In some form, believed to be prior to the
3rd century B.C.

INGREDIENTS: Macaroni, grated cheese with a sauce of butter, egg,
milk, cream, salt, pepper.

MAKERS: Various

NOTES: It was thought that Marco Polo brought Chinese "spaghetti"
to Italy, but macaroni-making tools are seen in the frescoes of Etruscan
tombs. The Etruscans are now believed to have migrated to Italy
from Lydia (in Asia Minor) about the 12th century B.C.

Reddi Wip®

DIMENSIONS: 1 qt. can: 8⁵⁄₁₆″ H × 2¹¹⁄₁₆″ Diam.

PACKAGE: Metal aerosol can, plastic cap. Printed offset lithography.

ORIGINATOR: Marcus Lipsky

DATE OF ORIGIN: 1948

INGREDIENTS: Pasteurized and homogenized cream, nonfat milk solids, sugar, corn syrup, mono- and diglycerides, artificial flavor, carrageenan, nitrous oxide (whipping gas).

MAKER: Hunt-Wesson Refrigerated Foods Division, Fullerton, California

SLOGAN: "The Real Cream of Toppings"

NOTES: Reddi Wip® is used in place of the whipped cream handmade by beating heavy cream. The procedure for making whipped cream is not always successful. Sometimes the cream refuses to thicken, but more often it separates—turning into a bowl of butter and liquid when whipped an instant too long.

Hershey's® Milk Chocolate

DIMENSIONS: 1.2 oz. bar: 5¼″ L × 1⅞″ W × ¼″ H

PACKAGE: Unprinted inner wrap, 22 lb. glassine. Label: one side clay coated 55 lb. paper, printed one-color rotogravure.

ORIGINATOR: Milton Snavely Hershey

DATE OF ORIGIN: April 17, 1895

INGREDIENTS: Milk chocolate (milk chocolate contains sugar, milk, cocoa butter, and chocolate) with soya lecithin, an emulsifier, vanillin, an artificial flavoring.

MAKER: Hershey Chocolate Company, Hershey, Pennsylvania

SLOGAN: "The Great American Chocolate Bar"

NOTES: Chocolate comes from the white beans in the pods of the cacao tree. The beans, which turn brown when exposed to air, are fermented, dried, and roasted to bring out the chocolate flavor. Native to Brazil, cacao was brought to Europe by the Spanish conquistadores. It was a luxury item then. Chocolate was first manufactured in the United States in 1765. In 1812, Milton Hershey, then a caramel maker, saw some European chocolate-making machines and decided to try to mass produce the new Swiss milk chocolate in the form of an inexpensive candy bar that many people could afford. Hugely and quickly successful, Hershey determined to create a chocolate capital in the fields around the new factory in Pennsylvania. The town of Hershey was planned and built on a concept adopted much later for Brasilia, the built-from-scratch capital of Brazil—the original home of chocolate.

Chef Boy-ar-dee® Spaghetti & Meat Balls

DIMENSIONS: 15 oz. can: 4¾″ H × 3″ Diam.

PACKAGE: Steel can with paper label printed four-color offset lithography.

ORIGINATOR: Hector Boiardi (Chef Boy-Ar-Dee)

DATE OF ORIGIN: 1929

INGREDIENTS: Tomatoes, cooked enriched spaghetti, beef, water, salt, sugar, crackermeal, modified food starch, dextrose, wheat flour, onions, soy protein isolate, romano cheese made from cow's milk, monosodium glutamate, hydrolyzed plant protein, caramel coloring, flavorings, garlic, cysteine and thiamine hydrochlorides.

MAKER: American Home Foods, New York, New York

SLOGAN: "A Delicious Hot Meal with Meat"

NOTES: Signore Boiardi, only 9 years old when he began as a kitchen apprentice in Italy, worked his way up to be chef at many famous restaurants in Rome, Paris, and New York.

Later, at his own restaurant in Cleveland, Ohio, his special recipe for spaghetti and sauce was immediately successful and he began to sell it for home consumption. The operation grew from a little room above the restaurant to the large factories that today can his various pasta products. Chef Boiardi's picture still appears on the label of every can.

Coca-Cola®

DIMENSIONS: 10 oz. bottle: 7¼″ H × 2⅜″ Diam. at base

PACKAGE: Glass with metal cap, designed by Root Glass Company in 1916. Bottle shape was granted registration as a trademark in 1960.

ORIGINATOR: Dr. John Styth Pemberton

DATE OF ORIGIN: May 1886

INGREDIENTS: Carbonated water, sugar, caramel color, phosphoric acid, natural flavorings, caffeine.

MAKER: The Coca-Cola Company, Atlanta, Georgia

SLOGANS: "Delicious and Refreshing"; "The Pause That Refreshes"; "Things Go Better with Coke"; "Have a Coke and a Smile".

NOTES: Coca-Cola® was created in syrup form to be used at Atlanta soda fountains. However, in 1889 Asa G. Chandler bought the product from Dr. Pemberton (for about $2,300) and made such a success of it that by 1894 an enterprising dealer began to bottle a mixture of the syrup and carbonated water for sale outside the Atlanta area. Five years later Chandler sold exclusive rights to bottle and sell Coca-Cola in most of the United States to Benjamin Thomas and Joseph Whitehead. With the idea of locally owned and operated bottling plants established, Chandler eventually sold the company in 1919 to Ernest Woodruff, whose son Robert began marketing the drink throughout the world. It is now sold in more than 135 countries, at the rate of 233 million drinks a day.

The distinctive soda-fountain glass was adopted in 1929. The name "Coke®" first appeared on labels in 1941, and was registered in 1945. The Coca-Cola bottle is a familiar part of pop art and Coke is perhaps the single most representative product of American popular culture.

Coca-Cola and Coke are registered trademarks which identify the same product of The Coca-Cola Company.

M & M's® Chocolate Candies

DIMENSIONS: 16 oz. pkg.: 9½″ L × 5″ W × approx. 1¾″ H

PACKAGE: Paper, printed four colors.

ORIGINATOR: Forrest E. Mars, Sr.

DATE OF ORIGIN: 1941

INGREDIENTS: Milk chocolate, sugar, corn starch and syrup, dextrin, artificial colors. (Milk chocolate contains sugar, milk, chocolate, cocoa butter, peanuts, emulsifier, salt, artificial flavors.)

MAKER: M & M/Mars, Division of Mars, Inc., Hackettstown, New Jersey

SLOGAN: "The Milk Chocolate Melts in Your Mouth—Not in Your Hand"

NOTES: M & M's® name comes from the initials of Forest Mars, Sr. and his then associate, Bruce Murrie. These confections withstand extreme climates and so they can be consumed anywhere in the world, a fact appreciated by servicemen in World War II. About 40 billion plain M & M's and 11 billion peanut M & M's are made in an average year.

Chun King® Chicken Chow Mein

DIMENSIONS: 28 oz. can: (overall) 7⅞″ H × 4″ Diam.

PACKAGE: Cans: Steel, with label of 60 lb. coated-one-side paper, printed four-color offset lithography, designed by Peterson & Blyth Associates.

ORIGINATOR: Jeno F. Paulucci

DATE OF ORIGIN: 1947

INGREDIENTS: Water, bean sprouts, celery, chicken meat, water chestnuts, carrots, bamboo shoots, modified food starch, mushrooms, sweet red peppers, pea pods, chicken fat, salt, sugar, hydrolyzed plant protein, monosodium glutamate, flavoring, spice, caramel color.

MAKER: RJR Foods, Inc., Winston-Salem, North Carolina

SLOGAN: "Good Tastes From the Good Earth"

NOTES: "Chow mein" means fried noodles and is one of the most popular of the many Chinese noodle dishes. It is from the Cantonese school—lightly cooked with light sauces.

Chun King Chow Mein began when Jeno Paulucci bought 25 pounds of bean sprouts and began production in a converted World War II Quonset hut in Duluth, Minnesota. The brand name was taken from Chungking, in Szechuan Province, the wartime capital of China.

Gelatin Dessert

ORIGINATOR: P. Cooper

DATE OF ORIGIN: 1845 patent. Described as "A transparent concentrated substance containing all the ingredients fitting it for table use in a potable form, and requiring only the addition of hot water to dissolve it so that it may be poured into moulds, and when it is cold will be fit for use."

INGREDIENTS: Gelatin, fruit juice (sugar and artificial coloring usually added in commercial products).

MAKERS: Various

NOTES: Gelatin, produced from a substance contained in bone, cartilage, and tendons, has been known for hundreds of years and is used to thicken broth and juices. The substance is also used to make capsules for medicines and vitamins, and for certain products of the photographic industry. Around the end of the nineteenth century Cooper's dessert idea was refined and made available commercially. In 1919, food chemist Joseph H. Cohen developed a gelatin that is the basis for a large part of the modern sparkly, brightly colored gelatin desserts that come packaged in powder form.

Chocolate Chip Cookies

DIMENSIONS: Approx. 2″ to 7″ Diam.

PACKAGE: Various

ORIGINATOR: Unknown. American version, Mrs. Wakefield.

DATE OF ORIGIN: American version, circa 1930.

INGREDIENTS: Butter, sugar, eggs, salt, baking soda, flour, vanilla, chocolate bits, nuts.

MAKERS: Various

NOTES: The word "cookie" comes from the Dutch *koekji*, a diminutive of *koek* (cake). Easy to store and carry, cookies are very popular in the United States. Motorized cookie carts and wagons travel the streets, there are "cookies-only" stores, and serious debates are conducted over the merits of various recipes. "Caught with your hand in the cookie jar" is an American folk expression meaning to be caught in the act of stealing.

There are thousands of cookie recipes, but chocolate chip cookies reign supreme. The original Toll House® chocolate chip recipe, belonging to the Nestlé Company, was developed about 50 years ago by Mrs. Wakefield, then owner of the Toll House Inn in Whitman, Massachusetts. (Chocolate chip cookies are also known as Toll House cookies). She added bits of semisweet chocolate to the American dropped butter cookie recipe. The result was so popular that chocolate companies began to score their bars and enclose a special chocolate chopper. Later, tiny morsels were packaged by Nestlé especially for the recipe.

Wise® Potato Chips

DIMENSIONS: 4½ oz. pkg.: 12½″ H × 6½″ W × 3″ D
PACKAGE: Plastic, printed in three colors
ORIGINATOR: Earl V. Wise, Sr.
DATE OF ORIGIN: 1921
INGREDIENTS: Potatoes, vegetable oil (may contain one or more of the
   following: cottonseed, palm, corn, partially hydrogenated soybean,
   partially hydrogenated cottonseed), salt.
MAKER: Borden's Inc., Columbus, Ohio
SLOGAN: "Still Made the Original Natural Way"

Baby Ruth® Candy Bar

DIMENSIONS: 2 oz. pkg.: 7″ L × 1¾″ W × 1¼″ D

PACKAGE: Paper, printed in two colors.

ORIGINATOR: Otto Schnering

DATE OF ORIGIN: 1920

INGREDIENTS: Sugar, roasted peanuts, corn syrup, hydrogenated vegetable oil (contains one or more of the following: palm kernel, coconut, soybean, palm, cottonseed, safflower oil), skim milk, soy flour, dextrose, whey, cocoa (processed with alkali), salt, natural flavors, sorbitol, lecithin and mono- and diglycerides (emulsifiers), sodium caseinate (protein), artificial flavors, dipotassium phosphate (buffer), artificial colors, calcium carrageenan (stabilizer).

MAKER: Curtiss, a Division of Standard Brands, Inc., New York, New York

SLOGANS: "When You Gotta Have One, You Gotta Have One"; "The Bigger, Better Candy Bar".

NOTES: Originally called Kandy Kake, the nut roll was renamed Baby Ruth in the mid twenties. Contrary to popular belief, it was not Babe Ruth but President Grover Cleveland's first daughter, known as "Baby Ruth", who was the inspiration.

Baby Ruth bars were publicized by a 26-plane aerial circus, a Scottish Kiltie Band, a Baby Ruth racing speedboat, hockey and bowling teams, and a six-pony team. In 1924, thousands of the bars, suspended from tiny parachutes, were dropped from airplanes over Pittsburgh. Baby Ruths were carried by MacMillan to the North Pole in 1927; by Admiral Byrd to the South Pole two years later. A song, "A Rose and a Baby Ruth", sold more than a million copies.

Oscar Mayer Wieners

DIMENSIONS: 16 oz. pkg.: 5″ L × 4″ W × 1⅝″ H

PACKAGE: Tri-layer plastic film package designed by Oscar Mayer Research Dept. Heatsealed paper band printed by color offset lithography, designed by Oscar Mayer Graphic Art Department.

ORIGINATOR: Oscar F. Mayer

DATE OF ORIGIN: October 1883

INGREDIENTS: Pork, water, beef, salt, corn syrup, flavoring, dextrose, sodium ascorbate (vitamin C), sodium nitrite.

MAKER: Oscar Mayer & Co., Madison, Wisconsin

SLOGAN: "Oh, I wish I were an Oscar Mayer Weiner.
That is what I'd truly like to be,
'cause if I were an Oscar Mayer Weiner,
everyone would be in love with me."

NOTES: Wursts originated in Austria and Germany (frankfurters come from Frankfurt), but the modern "hot dog" began as a "dachshund sausage" at Coney Island in 1871. It was then customary to eat wursts while holding them in one's fingers (it still is in Germany). As a refinement, hot dog concessions began to provide white gloves for customers. The first buns appeared in 1904 at the St. Louis "Louisiana Purchase Exposition" to replace the white gloves (customers were walking off with them). The term "hot dog" was coined in 1901 at the N.Y. Polo Grounds by cartoonist Tod Dorgan. He sketched some barking sausages in a roll—his version of the red hot "dachshund sausages" being sold. Since he couldn't spell dachshund he labeled them hot dogs.

French's Pure Prepared Mustard

DIMENSIONS: 6 oz. jar 3¼″ H × 2⅞″ Diam.

8 oz. bottle: 5½″ H × 2⅞₁₆″ Diam. at widest point

PACKAGE: Low density polyethylene, printed three-color gravure. Designed by Robert R. Mitchell Associates. "Therimage" decaltype label designed by Duncan M. Campbell, R. T. French Package Design Dept.

ORIGINATOR: George J. French

DATE OF ORIGIN: 1904

INGREDIENTS: Vinegar and water, mustard seed, salt, tumeric, spices, natural flavor.

MAKER: The R.T. French Company, Rochester, New York

SLOGANS: "French's, the Sunshine Mustard"; "Good Things to Eat Come From One Mustard Street".

NOTES: The mustard seed belongs to a large family of herbs, including turnip, horseradish, and watercress. Mustard was known in ancient times and is mentioned in the Bible (Luke, Matthew). The mustard seed is a symbol of faith.

French's product was first sold in 1904, the same year that hot dogs were introduced at the St. Louis World's Fair.

Jiffy Pop® Popcorn

DIMENSIONS: 5 oz. pan: 12″ L incl. handle × 7″ Diam. × ¹⁵⁄₁₆″ D

PACKAGE: Aluminum and aluminum foil, double polyboard, printed five-color offset lithography.

ORIGINATOR: Fred Mennen

DATE OF ORIGIN: Circa 1958

INGREDIENTS: Popcorn, partially hydrogenated vegetable oil shortening (contains one or more of the following: soybean oil, cottonseed oil, palm oil), salt.

MAKER: American Home Foods, New York, New York

SLOGAN: "Jiffy Pop Popcorn—Simple to Make, Tasty to Eat"

NOTES: Archaeological evidence of popcorn has been found in Central America dating back 7,000 years. A native American grain, the popcorn plant is somewhat smaller than the rest of the corn family and is thought to be the first corn to have been eaten.

Popcorn contains 13.5% moisture. When it is heated to 400°F the moisture changes into steam, building up pressure inside the hard kernel until finally the kernel bursts and the white insides pop out.

Heinz Kosher Dill Pickles

DIMENSIONS: 32 oz. jar: 6¼" H × 4⅛" Diam.

PACKAGE: Glass jar, metal cap. Paper label printed four-color offset lithography, designed by Heinz.

ORIGINATOR: Henry John Heinz

DATE OF ORIGIN: Pickles, 1869; Kosher dills, 1950

INGREDIENTS: Cucumbers, distilled vinegar, water, salt, garlic, spices, calcium chloride, natural flavorings, tumeric oleoresin, polysorbate 80, artificial color.

MAKER: H. J. Heinz Co., Pittsburgh, Pennsylvania

SLOGAN: "We've Got Your Pickle"

NOTES: Before refrigeration, pickling (curing in brine) was widely used to preserve food, but it also happened to make things tasty. H. J. Heinz created the small green replica of a pickle; first a plastic charm and then the Heinz Pickle Pin, a company symbol for nearly a century. The first ones were given away at the 1893 Chicago World's Fair and, by now, millions have been distributed.

Eggo® Frozen Waffles

DIMENSIONS: 11 oz. box: 9⅝" L × 4¾" W × 2⅝" H

PACKAGE: Cartonboard, printed four-color offset lithography, designed by Leo Burnett Company, Chicago

ORIGINATOR: Fearn Research

DATE OF ORIGIN: 1935

INGREDIENTS: Enriched wheat flour, water, partially hydrogenated vegetable oil (one or more of: soybean, palm, cottonseed), eggs, sugar, whey, baking powder, salt, vitamin A palmitate, reduced iron, niacinamide, artificial coloring, riboflavin (B_2), thiamin hydrochloride (B_1).

MAKER: Eggo Foods Division, Fearn International Inc., a subsidiary of the Kellogg Company, Franklin Park, Illinois

SLOGAN: "Leggo My Eggo"

NOTES: A waffle is a batter cake, crisper than a pancake, cooked in a special waffle iron. This device has two heated surfaces that make indentations in a grid pattern on the waffle as it bakes between them. The first waffle iron patent was taken out in the United States by Cornelius Swarthout on August 24, 1869. Waffle mixes in powdered form appeared around the turn of the century. Frozen waffles were among the first frozen foods. Primarily a breakfast food, waffles are also eaten for dessert, often with strawberries and whipped cream.

Budweiser® Beer

DIMENSIONS: 12 oz. bottle: 7⅞″ H × 2⅝″ Diam.

PACKAGE: Glass with metal cap. Paper label printed offset lithography, designed by Carl Conrad.

ORIGINATOR: Adolphus Busch

DATE OF ORIGIN: 1876

INGREDIENTS: Water, barley malt, rice, hops, yeast.

MAKER: Anheuser-Busch, Inc., St. Louis, Missouri

SLOGANS: "King of Beers"; "When You Say Bud, You've Said It All"; "This Bud's For You".

NOTES: Beer dates back at least to ancient Egypt, but it was not made commercially until the late Middle Ages. Ale once meant beer with no hops (a slightly bitter flavoring agent), but now means a pale malt drink *with* hops. *Lager* in German means storage place, and lager beers are stored for weeks or months before being sold. Bock is a heavier beer drunk at springtime. Porter is a strong, dark ale, and stout is even stronger, with more malt and hops.

Budweiser® was the first bottled beer sold nationally in the United States. It won Gold Medals for Lager Beer at World's Fairs: Paris 1878, Amsterdam 1883, New Orleans 1884–5, Chicago 1893, Vienna 1898, St. Louis 1904, Berlin 1908, and a Certificate of Merit at Melbourne 1888, and Prague 1903.

Planters® Dry Roasted Peanuts

DIMENSIONS: 12 oz. jar: 7½" H × 3½" Diam.

PACKAGE: Glass, with metal cap. Paper label printed three colors.

ORIGINATOR: Amedeo Obici

DATE OF ORIGIN: Circa 1910

INGREDIENTS: Peanuts, with added salt, modified food starch, gum arabic and/or dextrin, monosodium glutamate, yeast, paprika, and other spices, natural flavors.

MAKER: Planters, a Division of Standard Brands, New York, New York

SLOGAN: "Nutritious Planters"

TRADEMARK: Mr. Peanut®

NOTES: Native to South America, peanuts were brought to Africa and returned to North America via the slave trade. In the United States, less than 20% of the crop is eaten as peanuts. Hundreds of other uses were found by George Washington Carver, a black agricultural scientist who devoted his life to improving the economy of the South. Among these are cooking oil, soap, and, of course, peanut butter. The herbage is used for livestock feed.

The familiar cartoon character, Mr. Peanut®, came from a 1916 contest to select a trademark. The winner was a schoolboy's sketch of an animated peanut. The cane, top hat, and monocle were added later.

Good Humor® Ice Cream Sandwich

DIMENSIONS: Box of 12: 6¼″ L × 5¼″ W × 1¾″ H
Sandwich: 5″ L × 1⅞″ W × 1″ H

PACKAGE: 18 pt. board, printed offset lithography, designed by Lipton Graphics.

ORIGINATOR: Harry Burt

DATE OF ORIGIN: Circa 1950

INGREDIENTS: Sandwich: Enriched bleached flour, sugar, vegetable shortening (contains one or more of the following oils: partially hydrogenated soybean, palm, cottonseed, hydrogenated palm), corn syrup, artificial color, cocoa, baking soda, salt, lecithin, artificial flavors. Ice cream: milk fat and nonfat milk, sugar, corn syrup, whey, dextrose, vanilla extract, mono- and diglycerides, guar gum, locust bean gum, calcium carrageenan.

MAKER: Good Humor, Inc., Fairfield, New Jersey

SLOGANS: "America Loves Good Humor"

NOTES: Harry Burt began the Good Humor Company in 1920 when he succeeded in creating a chocolate-covered ice cream product. It was actually his young son, Harry, Jr., who suggested using a stick to keep the chocolate from melting in the hand, thus solving the main problem. This innovative product, combined with the novel idea of selling it from bicycle wagons announced by a distinctive chime, established Good Humor as a household word. The next breakthrough was the ice cream sandwich, which has carried on Good Humor popularity for the last three decades.

Vanilla Ice Cream
Sandwich
Good
Humor®
6 Sandwiches
NET CONTENTS: 6-2.5 FL. OZ. ICE CREAM
PLUS 2 WAFERS (15 FL. OZ. PLUS 12 WAFERS)

Campfire® Marshmallows

DIMENSIONS: 16 oz. bag: 11″ L × 6½″ W × approx. 3″ H

PACKAGE: Polyethylene bag printed by flexo or gravure, designed by Thomas Sheibley.

ORIGINATOR: Unknown

DATE OF ORIGIN: Campfire Marshmallows first sold circa 1900

INGREDIENTS: Corn syrup, sugar, water, cornstarch, dextrose, gelatin, modified soy protein, artificial flavor, sodium hexametaphosphate (improves texture), artificial color.

MAKER: Cracker Jack-B, Borden, Inc., Columbus, Ohio

SLOGANS: "One Taste Invites Another"; "Campfire, the Original Food Marshmallow".

NOTES: The marshmallow confection was originally made from the root of the marsh mallow, a plant native to Europe and a member of the mallow family of herbs and shrubs, many of which grow in marshy areas. Some other family members are cotton, rose of Sharon, okra, and hollyhock.

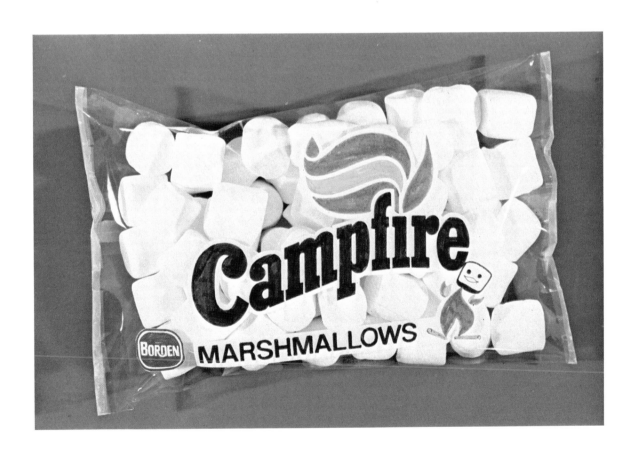

Kellogg's Froot Loops®

DIMENSIONS: 12 oz. box: $10^{15}\!/_{16}''$ H $\times$ $7^{9}\!/_{16}''$ W $\times$ $2^{11}\!/_{16}''$ D

PACKAGE: Cartonboard, printed four-color rotogravure, designed by Leo Burnett Company.

ORIGINATOR: Kellogg research team

DATE OF ORIGIN: 1963

INGREDIENTS: Sugar, corn, wheat and oat flour, partially hydrogenated vegetable oil (one or more of: cottonseed, coconut, soybean, palm), salt, artificial coloring, sodium ascorbate (C), vitamin A palmitate, niacinamide, ascorbic acid (C), natural orange, lemon, cherry with other natural flavorings, zinc oxide, reduced iron, thiamin hydrochloride (B_1), pyridoxine hydrochloride (B_6), riboflavin (B_2), folic acid, vitamin D_2, preservative BHA.

MAKER: Kellogg Company, Battle Creek, Michigan

NOTES: Cereal, a grain product, is one of man's oldest foods. Ancient cereals were whole grains and had to be cooked long to soften them and make them palatable, but they were the nutritional base of the time. Roman soldiers are said to have been able to conquer the world only with the help of their *polenta*, a combination of grains cooked together.

SPAM® Luncheon Meat

DIMENSIONS: 12 oz can: 3¾″ L × 3¼″ W × 2⅛″ H

PACKAGE: Metal, printed four-color offset lithography.

ORIGINATOR: George A. Hormel & Co.

DATE OF ORIGIN: 1937

INGREDIENTS: Chopped pork shoulder meat with ham meat added and salt, water, sugar, sodium nitrite.

MAKER: George A. Hormel & Co., Austin, Minnesota

SLOGANS: "The Meat of Many Uses by Hormel"; "A Lot of Meals. But Not a Lot of Money"; "There's a World of Things You Can Do With SPAM".

NOTES: According to *The Wall Street Journal*, the name SPAM® comes from the SP of spices and the AM of ham. The name became a household (and foxhole) word throughout the world in World War II. The product's cooked-in-the-tin process gave it a seven-year shelf life that made it ideal for wartime use. SPAM'S dignity suffered a bit from overexposure, as it was the object of many GI jokes, but the publicity kept sales at a high level even after the war. Krushchev himself paid tribute to the product without which ". . . we would not have been able to feed our army".

French's Idaho® Mashed Potatoes

DIMENSIONS: 13¾ oz. box: 7″ H × 5½″ W × 1⅝″ D

PACKAGE: Cardboard carton and paper/foil laminated inner pouches, printed four-color offset lithography, designed by Ed C. Kozlowski Designs.

ORIGINATOR: Dr. John Fogelberg invented the flexible innerpack and nitrogen packing system.

DATE OF ORIGIN: October 1946

INGREDIENTS: Dehydrated Idaho® potatoes 99%, vegetable monoglyceride, sodium phosphate, sodium sulfite, BHA and BHT added to preserve quality.

MAKER: The R. T. French Company, Rochester, New York

SLOGAN: "Tastes Like Idaho"

NOTES: Potatoes were grown by the Incas in Peru and brought to Europe by Spanish explorers. Mashed potatoes (also called purée) are a favorite form, but take a lot of work. Instant mashed potatoes need no peeling, mashing, or cooking. French's was the first instant mashed potato in the world for retail sale.

Del Monte Sliced Peaches

DIMENSIONS: 16 oz. can: 4⅜″ H × 3⅛″ Diam.

PACKAGE: Tin-lined steel can. Paper label, printed offset lithography,
designed by Logan, Carcy & Rehag.

ORIGINATOR: Oakland Preserving Company

DATE OF ORIGIN: 1892

INGREDIENTS: Peaches, water, sugar, corn sweetener.

MAKER: Del Monte Corporation, San Francisco, California

SLOGAN: "Good Things Happen When You Bring Del Monte Home"

NOTES: The peach is thought to have originated in China about 2,500 years
ago. To the Chinese, its pink blossom is a symbol of longevity. Peaches
were introduced into Persia and then were spread throughout Europe
by the Romans. Spaniards brought the peach to North America.

Peaches were one of the first hermetically preserved foods. They
were packed in France in 1810 by Nicolas Appert, who opened the first
commercial cannery in the world. Packed in glass until the 1850s, they
began being packed in tin by Francis Cutting of San Francisco in
the 1860s.

Oreo® Cookies

DIMENSIONS: 15 oz. bag: 7″ L × 5½″ W × 1⅞″ H

PACKAGE: Polypropylene, printed letterpress, paper labels designed by Lister/Butler.

ORIGINATOR: National Biscuit Company

DATE OF ORIGIN: March 6, 1912

INGREDIENTS: Sugar, enriched wheat flour (contains niacin, reduced iron, thiamine mononitrate [vitamin B_1], riboflavin [vitamin B_2], vegetable and/or animal shortening (lard and/or partially hydrogenated soybean oil and/or palm oil), cocoa (processed with alkali), corn sweetener, corn flour, whey, cornstarch, chocolate, sodium bicarbonate, salt, artificial flavor, lecithin.

MAKER: Nabisco, Inc., East Hanover, New Jersey

SLOGAN: "Oreo—America's Favorite Cookie"

NOTES: The word *oreo* means hill in Greek, and the Oreo Cookie, though always round, was more mound-shaped during testing and early production. Variations were introduced—a vanilla Oreo, a single cracker Oreo, and a lemon-filled Oreo (1920)—but the chocolate sandwich Oreo has emerged as the classic. It has been immortalized in plastic replicas used as costume jewelry (so realistic that people sometimes try to eat them). Oreo was known to be a favorite of the late Vice President Nelson Rockefeller.

Minute Maid® Frozen Concentrated Orange Juice

DIMENSIONS: 12 oz. can: 4⅞″ H × 2¹¹⁄₁₆″ Diam.

PACKAGE: Spiral wound paperboard with steel top and bottom. 60 lb. coated label printed three-colors rotogravure, designed by Dickens Design Group

ORIGINATOR: Minute Maid research and development team

DATE OF ORIGIN: Circa 1946

INGREDIENTS: 100% orange juice

MAKER: The Coca-Cola Company, Foods Division, Houston, Texas

SLOGANS: "If It's Minute Maid, There's No Doubt About It"; "Minute Maid, the Juices of Juice"; "Make Sure, Make It Minute Maid".

NOTES: Oranges originated in China and Indonesia. Columbus brought orange trees to the West Indies, and oranges were growing in Florida by 1565, in California by 1800. The blossoms are the state flower of Florida. There are at least four American cities named Orange, and one principality in southeast France, an earldom from the time of Charlemagne.

Frozen concentrated orange juice was developed by the Minute Maid Company as a result of an effort by the United States Army, during World War II, to provide soldiers in the field with a powder they could easily carry and mix with water to make orange juice. The war ended a few weeks after the powder was developed, so the company turned to making the frozen concentrate instead.

Kellogg's Corn Flakes®

DIMENSIONS: 8 oz. box: 9½″ H × 6¾″ W × 2⅜″ D

PACKAGE: Cartonboard, printed four-color letterpress.

ORIGINATOR: Will Keith Kellogg

DATE OF ORIGIN: April 1906

INGREDIENTS: Milled corn, sugar, salt, malt flavoring, sodium ascorbate (C), vitamin A palmitate, niacinamide, ascorbic acid (C), reduced iron, pyridoxine hydrochloride (B_6), thiamin hydrochloride (B_1), riboflavin (B_2), folic acid, vitamin D_2, BHA added to preserve product freshness.

MAKER: Kellogg Company, Battle Creek, Michigan

SLOGAN: "The Original Has This Signature" (referring to W.K. Kellogg's signature on box front)

NOTES: Will Keith Kellogg and his brother, Dr. John Henry Kellogg, experimented with cereal foods that could be used at a health institute operated by the doctor. In 1898 they succeeded in creating wheat flakes and then corn flakes. W.K. Kellogg planned to start his own company in 1902, but a fire destroyed his brother's sanitarium and he put his personal ambitions aside to help him rebuild. Finally, on February 19, 1906, W.K. Kellogg's company, The Battle Creek Toasted Corn Flake Company, was born.

Welch's® Grape Jelly

DIMENSIONS: 12 oz. jar: 5¼″ H × 2⅞″ Diam.

PACKAGE: Glass with four-color paper label designed by Jerome Gould and Ampersand and Associates. Contributions made by Al Kuser.

ORIGINATOR: Dr. Thomas Bremwell Welch

DATE OF ORIGIN: 1923

INGREDIENTS: Grapes, corn sweetener, sugar, fruit pectin, citric acid, sodium citrate.

MAKER: Welch Foods, Inc., Westfield, New York

SLOGAN: "Quality Since 1869"

NOTES: Dr. Welch produced his first grape juice, Dr. Welch's Unfermented Wine, for local churches. Renamed Welch's Grape Juice, it was introduced nationwide at the 1893 Chicago's World Fair. The Concord Grape Jelly was created in 1923.

Aunt Jemima® Pancake & Waffle Mix

DIMENSIONS: 8⅛″ H × 6⅛″ W × 2″ D

PACKAGE: Chipboard. Label paper, coated one side, printed by offset lithography. Designed by Frank De Raffele.

ORIGINATORS: Christopher Rutt and Charles Underwood

DATE OF ORIGIN: 1890

INGREDIENTS: Enriched unbleached flour (flour, niacin, reduced iron, thiamine mononitrate, riboflavin), corn flour, oat flour, rye flour, dextrose, monocalcium phosphate (a leavening agent), salt, sodium bicarbonate (a leavening agent), corn syrup, solids, artificial coloring.

MAKER: The Quaker Oats Company, Chicago, Illinois

NOTES: Aunt Jemima pancake mix is one of the first "convenience" foods. It was developed by a journalist (Rutt) and a flour miller (Underwood). They wanted a name to suggest the finest cooking; Southern hospitality and cooking then being legendary and Southern black women reputed the best cooks in the land, they chose "Aunt Jemima", the name of a popular song of the day.

Pancakes have a long history. In England on Shrove Tuesday the church bells are rung as a signal to start making pancakes (the pancake bell). In Liberal, Kansas, a race is held on that day, with each runner carrying a pancake in a skillet. The winner must flip the pancake at least three times before crossing the finish line first.

Aunt Jemima® Syrup

DIMENSIONS: 12 oz. jar: 8⅛″ H × 3½″ W at base × 1⁵⁄₁₆″ D

PACKAGE: Plastic, printed in four colors. Plastic cap.

ORIGINATOR: The Quaker Oats Company

DATE OF ORIGIN: 1964

INGREDIENTS: Corn syrup (75.2%), sugar syrup (20.8%), maple sugar syrup (2.0%), corn syrup solids, cellulose gum, natural and artificial flavors, sodium benzoate and sorbic acid (preservatives), caramel color.

MAKER: The Quaker Oats Company, Chicago, Illinois

NOTES: Sugarcane has been cultivated in Asia since prehistoric times. Arab traders taught the Chinese how to refine sugar in the 16th century. During the Middle Ages, sugar, called the "Indian honeybearing seed", came to Europe where it was sold as a medicine or a luxury.

Maple syrup was first made by American Indians from the sap of sugar maple and black maple trees. It was the staple sweetener of the early settlers.

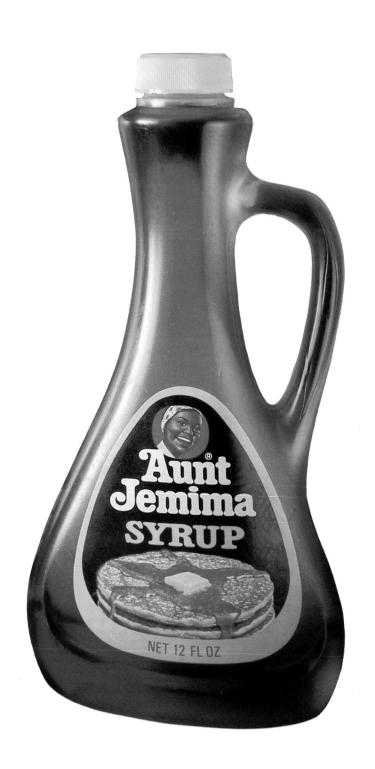

Snickers® Bar

DIMENSIONS: 1¹¹⁄₁₆ oz. pkg.: 5⅜″ L × 1¼″ W × ¾″ H

PACKAGE: Paper, printed color rotogravure.

ORIGINATOR: Frank C. Mars, Sr.

DATE OF ORIGIN: February 1930

INGREDIENTS: Sugar, peanuts, corn syrup, milk, cocoa butter, chocolate, butter, salt, emulsifier, egg whites, vegetable protein, natural and artificial flavors.

MAKER: M & M/Mars, Hackettstown, New Jersey

SLOGAN: "Packed with Peanuts, Snickers Really Satisfies"

Bazooka® Bubble Gum

DIMENSIONS: 1½" L × 1"W × ¼" D

PACKAGE: Waxed paper, printed in three colors.

ORIGINATOR: Unknown

DATE OF ORIGIN: Circa 1949

INGREDIENTS: Dextrose, sugar, corn syrup, gum base, softeners, natural and artificial flavors, artificial colors, BHT (to maintain freshness).

MAKER: Topps Chewing Gum, Brooklyn, New York

SLOGAN: "Young America's Favorite"

NOTES: Bubble gum must be flexible enough so that the tongue can push it forward to enable air to be blown into the pocket created. Brands vary and formulas are closely guarded secrets.

    The size of the biggest bubble ever blown is not certain, since bubble gum blowing contests abound. (There is even a set of rules available from the Bazooka company.) Records are not often kept, but one documented big bubble was 18¼" in diameter, blown at the Joe Garagiola/Bazooka Big League Bubble Gum Blowing Championship in 1975. Children are the primary users of bubble gum, often buying 25 to 50 pieces at a time, but 25% of the 68 million dollar bubble gum market belongs to adults, including some congressmen and movie stars.

Shown: Miss Anna Marta using the watermelon flavor.

Brownies

DIMENSIONS: Approx. 2½″ sq. × 1¼″ H

ORIGINATOR: Unknown

DATE OF ORIGIN: Unknown

INGREDIENTS: Chocolate, butter, sugar, eggs, salt, flour, vanilla, nuts.

MAKERS: Various

NOTES: Legend has it that brownies originated in a kitchen disaster turned triumph, when a cook's chocolate cake fell (or possibly never rose, since leavening agents were not very reliable until recently). Chocolate being expensive, the cook decided to save the costly failure and the cake was left to cool. Although rather flat, it looked appetizing enough, so the cook cut the layer into squares and tasted one. Rich, moist, rather chewy, it was a marvelous cross between cake, cookie, and candy. When the squares were served later, the delighted response led the cook to repeat the "disaster"—and brownies were born.

Hershey's® Kisses

DIMENSIONS: 14 oz. bag: 8″ L × 4¾″ W × approx. 1¼″ H

PACKAGE: Bag: polyethylene/polypropylene printed by reverse flexography. Wrap: .00035 aluminum foil with tissue plume printed by flexography.

ORIGINATOR: Milton Snavely Hershey

DATE OF ORIGIN: July 1, 1907. The plume was added August 8, 1921.

INGREDIENTS: Milk chocolate (contains sugar, milk, cocoa butter, and chocolate) with soya lecithin (an emulsifier), vanillin (an artificial flavoring).

MAKER: Hershey Chocolate Company, Hershey, Pennsylvania

SLOGAN: "A Kiss For You"

NOTES: Milton Hershey was owner of the Lancaster Caramel Company, which produced many caramel items, including "Hobson's Kisses" and "Massa's Kisses". He also produced chocolate novelties shaped like cigars, cigarettes, blossoms, and bicycles. The milk chocolate recipe worked out by Hershey was used to produce the beautifully shaped Hershey's® Kisses.

The Wrapped Kiss configuration is a registered trademark of Hershey Foods Corporation.

Wonder® Bread

DIMENSIONS : 12 oz. loaf: 10″ L × 4″ W × 4″ H

PACKAGE : Polyethylene, printed by flexography.

ORIGINATOR : Elmer Cline

DATE OF ORIGIN : July 13, 1921

INGREDIENTS : Enriched flour (barley malt, ferrous sulfate [iron], niacin [a B vitamin], thiamin mononitrate [B_1] riboflavin [B_2]), water, corn syrup, yeast, partially hydrogenated vegetable shortening (may contain soybean and/or cottonseed and/or palm oil), salt, soy flour, calcium sulfate, whey, wheat gluten, dough conditioners (may contain: sodium stearoyl-2-lactylate and/or mono- and diglycerides, and/or potassium bromate), calcium propionate (to retard spoilage). (Ingredients vary slightly across the United States. Those given here are used for the Northeast.)

MAKER : ITT Continental Baking Company, Rye, New York (Baking is done in 56 semi-autonomous bakeries throughout the country.)

SLOGANS : "Wonder Bread Builds Bodies 12 Ways", 1942-1971; "To Get Wonder Any Fresher You'd Have To Bake It Yourself", 1980.

NOTES : In large houses centuries ago, a butler gave bread to the diners according to their rank—the freshest bread for the master down to stale loaves for the lowest ranking. The 17th century introduced a new breakfast bread that was "toasted by fire and served with butter".

Wonder's balloon-decorated package was inspired by the thousands of balloons released into the air at the Indianapolis Speedway.

Campbell's Pork & Beans

DIMENSIONS: 16 oz. can: 4⅞″ H × 3″ Diam.

PACKAGE: Steel can with ¼ lb. tin coating. Paper label printed four-color offset lithography.

ORIGINATOR: Traditional American dish

DATE OF ORIGIN: Campbell's product first made in 1904.

INGREDIENTS: Prepared pea beans, water, tomato paste, sugar, corn syrup, pork, salt, modified food starch, distilled vinegar, natural flavoring, citric acid, oleoresin paprika.

MAKER: Campbell Soup Company, Camden, New Jersey

SLOGAN: "Rich Tomato Taste—a Campbell Tradition"

TRADEMARK: The Campbell Kids

NOTES: Campbell's Pork & Beans derive from a long tradition. Before Columbus reached America, the Indians had developed the pea bean used in pork and beans. Indian beans are known to have been used in the Massachusetts Bay colony in the 1630s and New England is still known for its bean dishes.

Campbell's is a trademark of Campbell Soup Company.

Cheez Doodles®

DIMENSIONS: 13½″ H × 6½″ W × 3½″ D

PACKAGE: Plastic, printed in five colors.

ORIGINATOR: The Yohi family

INGREDIENTS: Cornmeal, vegetable oil (may contain one or more of the following: cottonseed, coconut, palm, partially hydrogenated soybean), whey, salt, cheddar cheese, modified corn starch, artificial color, sodium caseinate, buttermilk, nonfat dry milk, monosodium glutamate (flavor enhancer), artificial flavors, ferric orthophosphate (source of iron), antolyzed yeast, ascorbic acid (vitamin C), niacin (a B vitamin), vitamin A palmitate, riboflavin (vitamin B_2), thiamine mononitrate (vitamin B_1).

MAKER: Borden Foods, Inc., Columbus, Ohio

NOTES: A blend of two of America's major food products, corn and cheese, this spiral shaped snack was conceived by the same people who produced the well-known Old London Melba Toast.

OVEN BAKED
FOR FLAVOR
PUFFED
cheez
doodles®
OR BEST FLAVOR USE
EFORE DATE SHOWN.
WISE®
BORDEN
cheez doodles®

Popsicle®

DIMENSIONS: Twin: 6″ L (incl. stick) × 2½″ W (at widest point × 1″ D
PACKAGE: Paper, printed two colors.
ORIGINATOR: Frank Epperson
DATE OF ORIGIN: Invented, 1905; patented, 1923.
INGREDIENTS: Water, sugar, corn syrup solids, citric acid (except
in banana and root beer), guar and carrageenan vegetable gums, salt,
artificial flavor (except orange, lemon, and lime which are natural
flavors), artificial color, (if chocolate, contains cocoa; if vanilla, contains
added nonfat milk solids).
MAKER: Popsicle Industries, Inc., Englewood, New Jersey
SLOGAN: "The Original Brand"
NOTES: In 1905, 11-year-old Frank Epperson left a mixture of powdered
soda mix and water on the back porch. Overnight, record low temperatures
made the stirring stick and mix freeze together, making the first
"Epsicle"—later to become Popsicle®. The Twin Popsicle® was created
in the Depression years to enable two children to share a Popsicle. In
World War II, an Eighth Air Force unit chose the Popsicle as its symbol
of American life. Popsicle has added to the original seven flavors until
now there are 34.
Flavors shown: Orange, cherry, and grape

McDonald's® Hamburgers

DIMENSIONS: Quarter Pounder: 2″ H × 4″ Diam.

ORIGINATORS: Maurice and Richard McDonald. Modified by Ray A. Kroc

DATE OF ORIGIN: 1948

INGREDIENTS: 100% pure beef pattie, sesame seed bun, ketchup, mustard, pickle, onion.

MAKER: McDonald's Corporation, Oak Brook, Illinois

SLOGAN: "Thick & Juicy, 100% Pure Beef"

NOTES: The original McDonald hamburger patties were made ten to the pound of beef. The Quarter Pounder, shown here, was introduced in 1971. Experiments were conducted to find the right wax paper to use between the patties. The paper has to be slick enough so that the meat will pop onto the grill and not stick to the paper, but not so slick as to make handling difficult.

One Midwest bakery—one of many making buns for McDonald's hamburgers—has a quarter-mile-long conveyor belt for cooling the buns and uses more than a million pounds of flour a month to make them.

McDonald's hamburgers are found in 6000 outlets in 25 countries. By 1980, 25 years after the founding of the chain by Ray Kroc, over 30 billion had been sold.

Heinz Tomato Ketchup

DIMENSIONS: 14 oz. bottle: 8¾" H × 2½" Diam. at widest point.

PACKAGE: Glass with metal cap. Paper labels printed in four colors, designed by Heinz.

ORIGINATOR: Henry John Heinz

DATE OF ORIGIN: 1867

INGREDIENTS: Red ripe tomatoes, distilled vinegar, corn sweetener, salt, onion powder, spice, natural flavoring.

MAKER: H.J. Heinz Company, Pittsburgh, Pennsylvania

SLOGANS: "The World's Largest Selling Ketchup"; "If It's Heinz, It's Got To Be Good."

NOTES: The Romans had a sauce called *garum* something like ketchup. The word "ketchup" came from the Chinese *ke-tsiap*, a brine of pickled fish or shellfish, and the Malaysian fish sauce *ki chop*. The English discovered the Malaysian sauce and tried to recreate it at home in the early 19th Century. It traveled to the United States, where tomatoes were added. (Tomatoes were not brought to the U.S. as a food plant until 1800. Although known in pre-Columbian Central and South America, tomatoes were grown in Spain only as ornaments, as they were thought to be poisonous.)

Bottles shown, left to right: ca. 1880, 1875, 1895-1900, 1914, current

McDonald's® French Fries

DIMENSIONS: Approx. 6½″ H × 5½″ W × 2½″ D

PACKAGE: Paperboard, printed rotogravure, designed by Diamond International.

ORIGINATORS: Maurice and Richard McDonald. Modified by Ray A. Kroc

DATE OF ORIGIN: 1948

INGREDIENTS: Russett Burbank potato, shortening, salt.

MAKER: McDonald's Corporation, Oak Brook, Illinois

SLOGAN: "World Famous Fries"

NOTES: Here is the secret of good french fries as it was discovered by Ray Kroc, founder of the McDonald's chain, at the first McDonald's restaurant in San Bernadino, California. The Idaho potatoes were piled in outdoor bins with walls of small mesh chicken wire. This kept the potatoes cool as they cured in the moving air. When the potatoes were peeled, a small amount of skin was left on. After being cut into narrow strips, they were gently washed in sinks of cold water to drain off excess starch, then given a final rinse with a spray hose. The potato strips in wire baskets were put into vats of pure unadulterated cooking oil and briefly fried. They were then drained, dried, and fried again to a golden brown, sprinkled with a bit of salt, then carefully put into bags, two or three at a time. Ray Kroc has remarked that the first success of the McDonald's restaurants was probably due to the excellence of their french fries. The method of preparation has been modified to accommodate large volume production.

A 1980 United States Government survey found that french fried potatoes are the most consumed vegetable in the nation.

Devil Dogs® Cakes

DIMENSIONS: Family pack: 6½″ L × 5¼″ W × 2⅝″ H

PACKAGE: Paper, printed offset lithography, designed by Chajet Design Group, Inc.

ORIGINATOR: Drake Bakeries

DATE OF ORIGIN: 1932

INGREDIENTS: Corn syrup, enriched flour (flour, niacin [a B vitamin], reduced iron, thiamine mononitrate [vitamin B_1], riboflavin [vitamin B_2]), partially hydrogenated vegetable shortening (contains one or more of the following: soybean oil, cottonseed oil, palm oil), whey, water, Dutch process cocoa (alkalized), soya flour, skim milk, eggs, carob powder, baking soda, sodium propionate (preserves freshness), salt, buttermilk, rye flour, sodium caseinate, mono- and diglycerides (emulsifier), sodium aluminum phosphate with aluminum sulfate (leavening), isolated soy protein, vanilla, calcium caseinate, sorbitan monostearate and polysorbate 60 (emulsifier), sorbic acid (preservative), vanillin (artificial flavor).

MAKER: Drake's Bakeries, Wayne, New Jersey

SLOGAN: "Bite a Devil Dog, It Won't Bite Back"

NOTES: The name Devil Dogs® comes from the product's being a devil's food cake shaped like a hot dog bun.

McDonald's® Milkshakes

DIMENSIONS: 5″ H × 3½″ Diam.

PACKAGE: Paper, waxed, printed two-color flexography. Lid not shown.

ORIGINATORS: Maurice and Richard McDonald. Modified by Ray A. Kroc

DATE OF ORIGIN: 1948

INGREDIENTS: Fresh whole milk or cream, nonfat milk, sugar, corn syrup, vanilla, stabilizer, flavoring.

MAKER: McDonald's Corporation, Oak Brook, Illinois

SLOGAN: "Triple Thick"

NOTES: It was the milkshake (not the hamburger) that brought about the McDonald's chain. Ray A. Kroc, founder of the present McDonald's company, previously sold Multimixers, a machine that mixed six milk shakes at one time. He first went to see the McDonald brothers at their drive-in restaurant in San Bernadino, California in 1954, after having heard that they had eight Multimixers in constant use. Kroc found there the prototype of stripped-down fast food operations that would later sweep the country. He had visions of many McDonalds' across the country, all with eight Multimixers, and proposed the idea to the McDonald brothers. Only after he volunteered to create and run the chain himself, did the McDonalds agree to the idea. Of course, the milkshakes today are made with much larger equipment than the Multimixer.

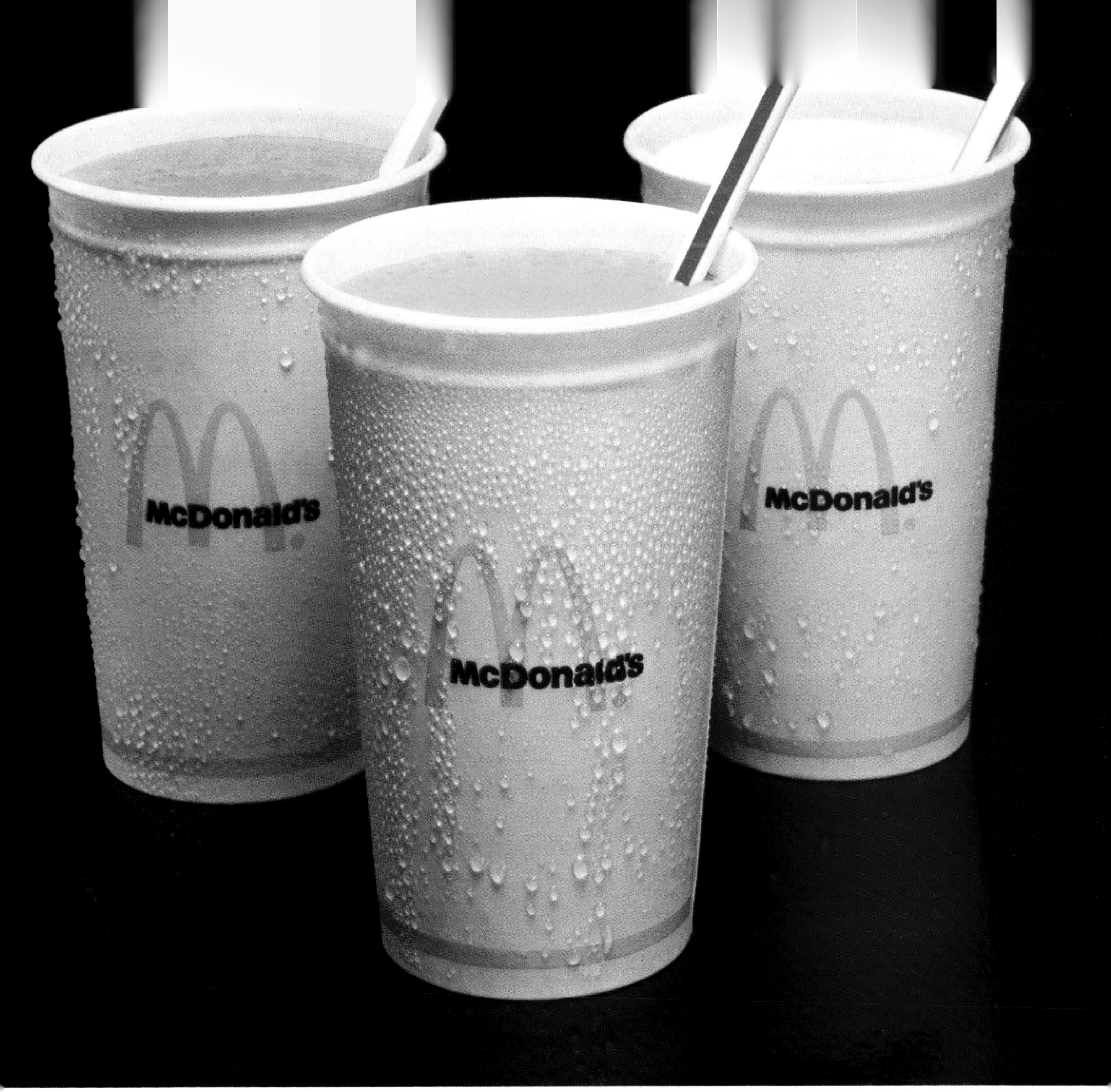
McDonald's
McDonald's
McDonald's

Tony's™ Pizza

DIMENSIONS: $10\frac{3}{4}''$ Diam. $\times$ $\frac{15}{16}''$ H

PACKAGE: Fiber tray, shrink wrapped film, unprinted with paper label, polycoat reverse side, printed four-color offset lithography, designed by Tony's Pizza Service.

ORIGINATOR: Unknown, traditional Italian dish

DATE OF ORIGIN: Unknown

INGREDIENTS: Pepperoni pizza: enriched flour, water, tomato paste, pepperoni (BHA, BHT with citric acid added to help protect flavor, pork and beef, salt, water, dextrose, spices, lactic acid starter culture, oleoresin of paprika, dehydrated garlic, sodium nitrite), cheddar cheese, low moisture-part skim mozzerella cheese, corn oil, salt, soybean oil, sugar, romano cheese (made from cow's milk), yeast, dough conditioner (whey, ammonium sulfate, L-cysteine), monosodium glutamate, calcium propionate, spices.

MAKER: Tony's Pizza Service, Marshall, Minnesota

SLOGANS: "Pizza Craver's Pizza"; "Ah Tony's, That's Some Kind of Pizza!"; "The Well-Rounded Meal".

NOTES: During World War II, large numbers of Americans became acquainted with pizza in the northeastern United States and in Italy. After the war, pizza parlors and stands appeared all over the country. Tony's Pizza brand originated in a Salinas, Kansas pizza parlor. The frozen version was created because customers wanted the convenience of having a pizza ready in the freezer for a late snack. Pizza began as a poor peasant's meal—a crust with some sauce and seasoning. The many varied toppings available today are comparatively recent innovations.

Cream Cheese

DIMENSIONS: Standard package: 2¾″ L × 2⅛″ W × ⅞″H

PACKAGE: Traditionally, aluminum foil lined with white paper.

ORIGINATOR: Unknown

DATE OF ORIGIN: Unknown

INGREDIENTS: Cultured milk, fresh cream, salt, enzymes, gum agent.

MAKERS: Various

NOTES: Any people with domestic animals to provide milk had cheese. Ancient Greeks used milk from mares and goats, Egyptians used camel milk, Laplanders have reindeer milk, and other countries use sheep, water buffalo, and, of course, cows to obtain milk for cheese. It takes about 100 lbs. of milk to make 10 lbs. of cheese.

Cream cheese is added to many recipes—from cream cheese spread to cheese cake desserts. Long ago, cream cheese was made at home ("Joy of Cooking" still describes how, if you'd like to try), but now there are many brands available in stores.

Cracker Jack®

DIMENSIONS: 1.13 oz. pkg.: 5″ H × 2¾″ W × 1⅛″ D

PACKAGE: Foil-wrapped paper box, printed offset lithography. Original box designed by F. W. Rueckheim, who also created Jack the Sailor Boy and Bingo, his dog.

ORIGINATOR: F. W. Rueckheim

DATE OF ORIGIN: 1872

INGREDIENTS: Sugar, corn syrup, popcorn, peanuts, molasses, vegetable oil, corn oil, salt, soya lecithin.

MAKER: Borden, Inc., Columbus, Ohio

SLOGANS: "The More You Eat the More You Want"; "America's Famous Confection".

NOTES: Mr. Rueckheim's creation, already popular in the Chicago area, was introduced to 21 million people at the 1893 Chicago World's Fair. The name Cracker Jack came later in 1896 when the snack was tasted by a salesman, who exclaimed, "That's a crackerjack!"—a slang expression of the day meaning something excellent. In 1908, the song "Take Me Out to the Ballgame" immortalized Cracker Jack, with the line "Buy me some peanuts and Cracker Jack". The famous toy surprise was introduced in 1912. In 1919, Jack, the little sailor, and his dog Bingo appeared on the package.

Shown: A 1934 Mystery Box, a classic with its own toy compartment.

Wrigley's Juicy Fruit Chewing Gum®

DIMENSIONS: Seven stick package: 2″ L ×⅞″ W × 11⁄16″ D

PACKAGE: Foil, paper, cellophane, printed rotogravure, designed by Wrigley Art Dept.

ORIGINATOR: William Wrigley, Jr.

DATE OF ORIGIN: 1893

INGREDIENTS: Sugar, gum base, corn syrup, dextrose, softeners, natural flavors.

MAKER: Wm. Wrigley Jr. Company, Chicago, Illinois

SLOGAN: "Flavor Lover's Gum"

NOTES: Ancient Greeks chewed resins from the mestic tree. The Mayans in Yucatan chewed chicle more than a thousand years ago. Gum from the resin of spruce trees was sold in the United States until the 1860s, when chicle was introduced. Gum base is a blend of latex products from trees in tropical rainforests. The milky white liquids ooze from slits in the trees and are boiled down and molded into blocks. These are ground, purified, dried, melted, and filtered. Sweetness and flavoring are added, then rolling machines flatten the mixture to form the familiar sticks. Commercial chewing gum originated in the United States, but is now sold in over 110 countries.

Hostess® Donuts

DIMENSIONS: Box: 9¾" L × 4¾" W × 3¼" H

PACKAGE: Paperboard, original designed by Roger Ferriter, line extensions designed by Frank Sessa.

ORIGINATOR: Unknown

DATE OF ORIGIN: 1930s

INGREDIENTS: Enriched flour (niacin [a B vitamin], reduced iron, thiamine mononitrate [B_1], riboflavin [B_2], partially hydrogenated vegetable and animal shortening (may contain soybean oil, cottonseed oil, palm oil, beef fat, lard), skim milk, dextrose, sugar, water, soy flour, starch, leavening (sodium acid pyrophosphate, baking soda, sodium aluminum phosphate), egg yolks, salt, rye flour, mono- and diglycerides, sodium caseinate, lecithin, fumaric acid, artificial color (Yellow 5) and flavor, potassium sorbate (to retard spoilage).
(Ingredients very slightly across the United States. Those shown here are used for the Northeast.)

MAKER: ITT Continental Baking Company, Rye, New York (Baking is done in 56 semi-autonomous bakeries throughout the country.)

SLOGAN: "Keep 'em Home for Breakfast with Hostess"

NOTES: Dutch settlers brought a round, fried *olykoeck* recipe to early America. Sea captain Hanson Gregory is credited with putting holes in doughnuts in 1847, on the theory that this would make them more easily digested. A bronze plaque records his birthplace near Rockport, Maine.

Nestlé's Taster's Choice® Freeze Dried Coffee

DIMENSIONS: 8 oz. jar: 6″ H × 4″ W × 2⅞″ D

PACKAGE: Glass, metal cap. Paper label printed five-color offset lithography, designed by Lippincott Margulies.

ORIGINATOR: Nestlé research and technological team

DATE OF ORIGIN: 1966

INGREDIENTS: 100% freeze-dried coffee.

MAKER: The Nestlé Company, Inc., White Plains, New York

SLOGAN: "It Looks, Smells, Tastes, Like Ground Roast Coffee"

NOTES: Coffee comes from the berries of an evergreen shrub which originally grew wild in Ethiopia. By the 13th century, *k'hawah* was used as a food, a medicine, and a beverage throughout Arabia. Coffee spread from there to Turkey about 1500 and to Italy and Europe in the 1600s. The beverage's popularity led to the development of coffeehouses as a social institution. Coffee was introduced to Brazil, now its leading producer, only in the 18th century.

Americans drink over 500 million cups each day, consuming one third of the world's supply. Freeze dried instant coffee is a recent development. Shown is the decaffeinated version.

The ancient Incas freeze dried their food for storage naturally, by exposing it alternately to the freezing night air and hot sun of the Andes.

Barnum's Animals® Crackers

DIMENSIONS: 2 oz. box: 2¾″ H × 5⅛″ W × 1⅝″ D

PACKAGE: Recycled paperboard, printed four-color offset lithography, designer unknown. Carrying string: cotton braided tape.

ORIGINATOR: Adapted from traditional English crackers.

DATE OF ORIGIN: 1902

INGREDIENTS: Enriched wheat flour (contains niacin, reduced iron, thiamine mononitrate [vitamin B_1], riboflavin [vitamin B_2]), sugar, corn sweetener, vegetable or animal shortening (partially hydrogenated soybean oil and palm oil or lard), corn flour, whey, salt, sodium bicarbonate, artificial flavor.

MAKER: Nabisco, Inc., East Hanover, New Jersey

NOTES: Named for circus impressario P.T. Barnum, Animal Crackers, in their colorful circus-wagon box with a carrying string at the top, first appeared as a Christmas season special, but soon became a year-round favorite. Universally popular, they gave the name to a Marx Brothers movie and one of the most successful songs sung by Shirley Temple, "Animal Crackers in My Soup".

Marshmallow Fluff®

DIMENSIONS: 7½ oz. jar: 5″ H × 3¼″ Diam.

PACKAGE: Glass, paper label, printed offset lithography

ORIGINATORS: H. Allen Durkee and Fred L. Mower

DATE OF ORIGIN: April 1920

INGREDIENTS: Cane sugar, corn syrup, dried egg white, artificial flavoring, cream of tartar.

MAKER: Durkee-Mower Inc., Lynn, Massachusetts

NOTES: Listed in the 1968 Griffin Report as number 13 of the 100 Best Selling Products in New England.

Candied Apples

DIMENSIONS: Approx. 7″ H incl. skewer × 3½″ Diam.

PACKAGE: Unprinted wax paper wrap. Wooden skewer.

ORIGINATOR: Unknown

DATE OF ORIGIN: Unknown. Traditional.

INGREDIENTS: Fresh whole apple, stick or skewer, syrup glaze
(light corn syrup, sugar, water, and red food coloring).

MAKERS: Various

NOTES: Candied apples are seen mostly in the fall at fairs and circuses
throughout America. Some people make them at home for Halloween
treats and parties. A variant, taffy apples, are caramel coated.

Apples are native to the Caucasus mountains in western Asia, and
have been cultivated since prehistoric times. There are thousands of
varieties. No one can say which one grew in the Garden of Eden and
some say that it was not an apple at all, but some other fruit.

Brach's® Candies

PACKAGES: Various

ORIGINATOR: Emil J. Brach

DATE OF ORIGIN: 1904

INGREDIENTS: Various

MAKER: E. J. Brach & Sons, Chicago, Illinois

SLOGAN: "Brach's, the Old-Fashioned Candy Store Candy"

NOTES: The old-fashioned candy store with its wide variety of candies in glass jars is behind the concept of Brach's candies. There are now over 200 different chocolate and non-chocolate candies in the Brach's line. Most familiar are the seasonal items, such as the Halloween candy corn. In 1945 Brach's switched from bulk candy to packaged candy in cellophane bags.

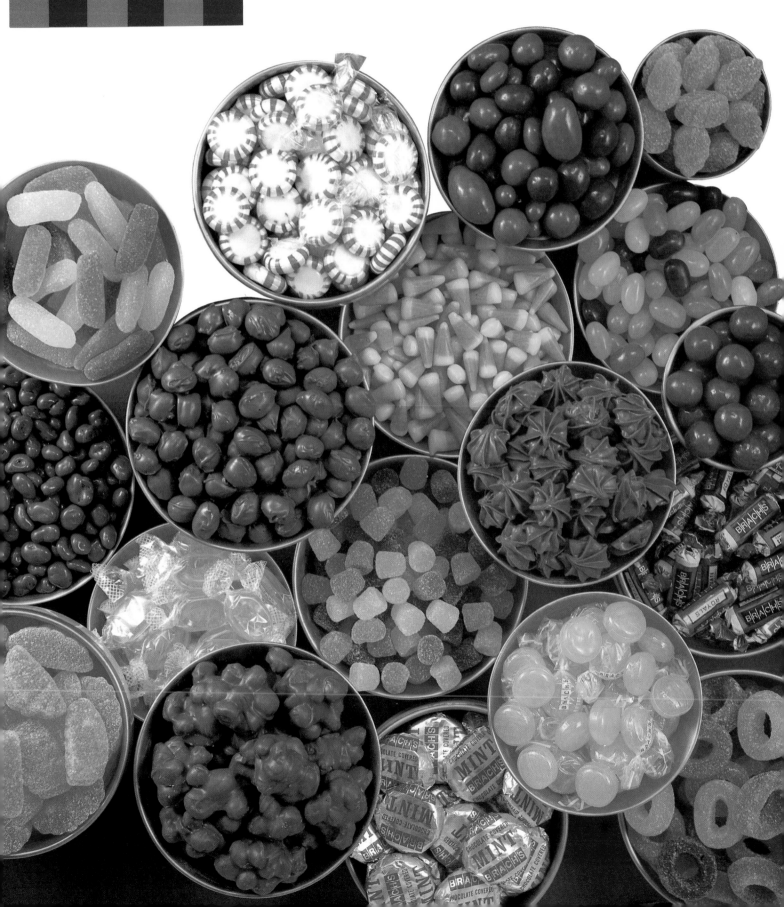

Tootsie Roll®

DIMENSIONS: 1⅜ oz. pkg.: 6″ L × ⅞″ Diam.

PACKAGE: Paper, printed in two colors, with board inside.

ORIGINATOR: Leo Hirschfield

DATE OF ORIGIN: 1896

INGREDIENTS: Sugar, corn syrup, condensed skim milk, partially hydrogenated soy or coconut oils, cocoa, whey, vegetable lecithin, artificial and natural flavors.

MAKER: Tootsie Roll Industries, Inc., Chicago, Illinois

NOTES: Austrian immigrant Leo Hirschfield hand rolled and wrapped his first candies, made from a recipe brought from Europe. They sold for one penny each. He named the candy "Tootsie Roll" after his little girl, whom he called "Tootsie".

Kentucky Fried Chicken®
Dinner

DIMENSIONS: Carton containing dinner: 7″ L × 4½″ W × 2¾″ H

PACKAGE: Double wrapped carton: solid bleached sulphate (paperboard). Printed two-color rotogravure, flexography, or letterpress.

ORIGINATOR: Colonel Harland Sanders

DATE OF ORIGIN: 1956

INGREDIENTS: Chicken fried under pressure in vegetable shortening in a Sanders-designed pot, with a formula of 11 herbs and spices.

MAKER: Kentucky Fried Chicken Corporation, Louisville, Kentucky

SLOGANS: "North America's Hospitality Dish"; "It's Finger Lickin' Good"; "It's Nice to Feel Good About a Meal".

NOTES: At age 66, Colonel Sanders began to franchise his method of frying chicken, using his own recipe. A personal appearance on a TV talk show made him a national symbol. His picture appears on all Kentucky Fried Chicken packages. The Colonel was still making commercials and traveling for the company at age 88.

It is said that if all the Kentucky Fried Chickens consumed in the world were laid end to end, they would stretch 93,000 miles, circling the earth about four times at the equator.

Hawaiian Punch®

DIMENSIONS: 46 oz. can: 6¾″ H × 4″ Diam.

PACKAGE: Steel can with label of 60 lb. coated-one-side paper, printed four-color offset lithography, designed by RJR Foods.

ORIGINATORS: A. W. Leo and Tom Yates

DATE OF ORIGIN: 1944

INGREDIENTS: Water, sugar and corn syrups, fruit juices and purées (concentrated pineapple, grapefruit, and orange juices, passionfruit juice, apricot, papaya, and guava purées), citric acid (provides tartness), natural fruit flavors, vitamin C, dextrin (a flavor carrier), artificial color, ethyl mattol (a flavor enhancer).

MAKER: RJR Foods, Inc., Winston-Salem, North Carolina

SLOGAN: "Fruit Juicy, Hawaiian Punch"

NOTES: Hawaiian Punch® was first produced as a concentrated beverage and sherbet base for southern California beverage fountains and ice cream manufacturers. In 1950, national distribution began with the introduction of ready-to-drink Hawaiian Punch in 46-ounce cans.

Hostess® Sno Balls

DIMENSIONS: Pkg. of two: 5¼″ L × 3″ W × 2¼″ H

PACKAGE: Polypropylene, printed by flexography. Logo designed by Walter Einsel.

ORIGINATOR: Ellis Baum

DATE OF ORIGIN: 1947

INGREDIENTS: Sugar, water, corn syrup, enriched flour (niacin [a B vitamin], reduced iron, thiamin mononitrate [B₁], riboflavin [B₂]), coconut, partially hydrogenated animal and vegetable shortening (may contain beef fat and/or lard and soybean and/or cottonseed and/or palm oil), skim milk, cocoa, gelatin, whey, leavening (sodium acid pyrophosphate, baking soda, monocalcium phosphate), salt, mono- and diglycerides, sodium caseinate, polysorbate 60, artificial color and flavor, sorbic acid (to retard spoilage). Ingredients vary slightly across the United States. (Those given here are used for the Northeast).

MAKER: ITT Continental Baking Company, Rye, New York (Baking is done in 56 semi-autonomous bakeries throughout the country.)

SLOGANS: "Freshness Never Tasted So Good"; "You Get a Big Delight In Every Bite"; "Hostess, Freshness, Kids . . . They Go Together"; "When I Say 'Yes', It's Hostess".

My*T*Fine® Instant Chocolate Pudding

DIMENSIONS: 4¼ oz. pkg.: 2⅞″ H × 3½″ W × 1⅜″ D

PACKAGE: Clay coated newsback, printed four-color offset lithography, designed by RJR Foods.

ORIGINATOR: D & C Flour Co.

DATE OF ORIGIN: Regular, 1918; Instant, 1945

INGREDIENTS: Sugar, modified food starch, cocoa processed with alkali, sodium phosphate, di- and monoglycerides, artificial flavor, color.

MAKER: RJR Foods, Inc., Winston-Salem, North Carolina

NOTES: Early cookery grouped dumplings and puddings together, probably because both were cooked by steaming. In fact, a very early use of the word pudding referred to sausages, as in black pudding or white pudding.

Puddings range from Yorkshire pudding—a batter baked under meats or in the juices—to Sussex—a dumpling filled with meat—to sweet, heavy puddings, like Christmas plum pudding, to the lighter dessert puddings of milk, eggs, thickeners, and flavorings that Americans think of as puddings.

Milky Way® Bar

DIMENSIONS: 5⅜″ L × 1¼″ W × ¾″ H

PACKAGE: Paper, printed color rotogravure.

ORIGINATOR: Frank C. Mars, Sr.

DATE OF ORIGIN: September 1923

INGREDIENTS: Milk chocolate, corn syrup, sugar, milk, partially hydrogenated vegetable oil (peanut, palm), cocoa, butter, salt, malt, egg white, vegetable protein, artificial flavor. (Milk chocolate contains sugar, milk, cocoa butter, chocolate, emulsifier, natural and artificial flavors.)

MAKER: M & M/Mars, Hackettstown, New Jersey

SLOGAN: "At Work, Rest, or Play, It Is You and MILKY WAY"

NOTES: Frank C. Mars and his friends loved chocolate malteds. He invented the Milky Way® bar to make the chocolate malted taste available in a candy.

Milk chocolate is created from chocolate "liquor" (cakes of the crushed, roasted meats inside the cocoa bean), cocoa butter, milk and sugar blended to dough-like consistency, then ground and refined to paste. The paste is put through a kneading action in shell-like containers (conches).

Swanson Turkey Dinner

DIMENSIONS: 16 oz. pkg.: 7⅛″ H × 9¹⁄₁₆″ W × 1″ D

PACKAGE: Paperboard, printed four-color offset lithography, designed by Campbell Soup Company, Swanson Division.

ORIGINATORS: W. Charles and Gilbert C. Swanson

DATE OF ORIGIN: Mid 1940s

INGREDIENTS: Turkey with gravy and dressing, whipped potatoes, peas and carrots in seasoned sauce, apple-cranberry cake cobbler.

MAKER: Campbell Soup Company, Camden, New Jersey

NOTES: The Swanson frozen dinners were created to help the servantless American housewife after World War II. New dishes were tested in the kitchens of C. A. Swanson & Sons and then submitted for approval to a panel of hotel chefs and 1,200 housewives. The first "TV Dinner" was turkey, the same dish used by the Pilgrims for their first Thanksgiving dinner over 300 years earlier.

Swanson is a trademark of Campbell Soup Co.

Hostess® Cup Cakes

DIMENSIONS: Pkg. of two: 5″ L × 2¼″ W × 2″ H

PACKAGE: Polypropylene, printed color flexography. Logo designed by Walter Einsel.

ORIGINATOR: D. R. (Doc) Rice

DATE OF ORIGIN: August 19, 1919

INGREDIENTS: Sugar, water, enriched flour (niacin [a B vitamin], reduced iron, thiamine mononitrate [B_1], riboflavin [B_2]), partially hydrogenated animal and vegetable shortening (may contain beef fat and/or lard or soybean and/or cottonseed and/or palm oil), corn syrup, skim milk, cocoa, whey, modified food starch, leavening (sodium acid pyrophosphate, baking soda, monocalcium phosphate), salt, chocolate, mono- and diglycerides, gelatin, sodium caseinate, polysorbate 60, agar, lecithin, artificial flavor, sorbic acid (to retard spoilage). (Ingredients vary slightly across the U.S. Those given here are used for the Northeast.)

MAKER: ITT Continental Baking Company, Rye, New York (Baking is done in 56 semi-autonomous bakeries throughout the country.)

SLOGANS: "Freshness Never Tasted So Good"; "You Get a Big Delight In Every Bite"; "Hostess, Freshness, Kids . . . They Go Together"; "When I Say 'Yes', It's Hostess".

NOTES: The chocolate cupcakes originated in 1919 were given their final embellishments—filling, icing, and a white squiggle— by "Doc" Rice in 1945.

Wheaties®

DIMENSIONS: 8 oz. box: 9%16″ H × 6¾″ W × 2″ D

PACKAGE: Paper cartonboard, printed in four colors.

ORIGINATOR: Washburn Crosby Company

DATE OF ORIGIN: 1924

INGREDIENTS: Whole wheat, sugar, salt, malt syrup, calcium carbonate, trisodium phosphate, sodium ascorbate (vitamin C), annatto extract color, niacinamide (a B vitamin), iron (a mineral nutrient), vitamin A palmitate, pyridoxine hydrochloride (vitamin B_6), thiamin mononitrate (vitamin B_1), riboflavin (vitamin B_2), cyanocobalamin (vitamin B_{12}), vitamin D_2. Freshness preserved with BHT.

MAKER: General Mills, Inc., Minneapolis, Minnesota

SLOGAN: "Breakfast of Champions"®

NOTES: Starting from an accidental spill of bran gruel onto a hot stove in 1921, a crispy, flaky bran cereal was developed. The name "Wheaties" was chosen through an internal company contest. Only modestly successful at first, Wheaties' sales were brought to life by the first singing commercial, on a Minneapolis-St. Paul radio station in 1926. Three years later, sales were down again and Wheaties almost went out of business. Radio advertising was expanded and Wheaties grew again. It sponsored the phenomenally successful show "Jack Armstrong, the All-American Boy", which began in 1933 and ran until 1951. Wheaties' advertising continues to be closely connected with physical fitness and sports.

Life Savers®

DIMENSIONS: Pep-O-Mint roll: 2⅞″ L × ¹¹⁄₁₆″ Diam. Five Flavor
roll: 2¹⁵⁄₁₆″ L × 1³⁄₁₆″ Diam.

PACKAGE: Foil and paper, printed by gravure, designed by Tom James,

ORIGINATOR: Clarence Crane

DATE OF ORIGIN: 1913

INGREDIENTS: Sugar, corn syrup, artificial and natural flavors,
artificial colors, stearic acid.

MAKER: Life Savers, Inc., New York, New York

SLOGANS: "The Candy With the Hole®"; "Life Savers, a Part of Living";
"Life Savers, They're Like Comin' Home".

NOTES: Launched as Crane's Life Savers, the product was purchased
soon after by Edward Noble and a partner. Noble dropped its cardboard
package design and adopted the present foil wrapper with a band, one
of the first uses of foil in packaging. A brilliant merchandiser, Noble
arranged to have Life Savers placed next to the cash register in stores.
Life Savers received five government "E" citations for excellence during
World War II, when billions of packages were shipped to the
Armed Forces.

Life Savers® Roll Candy is a registered trademark of Life Savers, Inc.

Ritz® Crackers

DIMENSIONS: 12 oz. box: 9″ H × 6⅜″ W × 2⅜″ D

PACKAGE: Clay coated recycled paperboard carton with paper cover printed four-color rotogravure.

ORIGINATOR: National Biscuit Company

DATE OF ORIGIN: 1934

INGREDIENTS: Enriched wheat flour (contains niacin, reduced iron, thiamine mononitrate [vitamin B_1], riboflavin [vitamin B_2]), vegetable and animal shortening (partially hydrogenated soybean oil or coconut oil, lard), sugar, corn sweetener, salt, malted barley flour, sodium bicarbonate, calcium phosphate.

MAKER: Nabisco, Inc., East Hanover, New Jersey

SLOGANS: "There Is Only One Ritz"; "Anytime Is The Right Time To Serve Ritz"; "Everything Tastes Great When It Sits On a Ritz".

NOTES: After years of experimenting to create a buttery cracker, the Ritz Cracker was born. With more shortening and no yeast, Ritz was crisper, less fluffy than other crackers on the market, and had a special taste. An instant success, over five million Ritz crackers were sold in the first year. Within three years it became a super-selling cracker, with 29 million baked daily. An extraordinary recipe sometimes printed on the box tells how to make a pie that tastes just like apple pie, but without any apples—with 36 Ritz Crackers instead.

NABISCO
RITZ CRACKERS
STACK PACK
RITZ
CRACKERS
...there is only one Ritz!
3 STACK PACKS
(Reclosable moisture-proof packs)
NET WT 12 OZ
340 GRAMS

Borden® American Pasteurized Process Cheese Food

DIMENSIONS: 16 oz. pkg.: 3½″ sq. × 2¼″ H

PACKAGE: Individual slices wrapped in heatsealed transparent film. Slices over-wrapped with heatsealed printed wrapper, designed by Blau Bishop & Associates.

ORIGINATOR: Borden Foods, Borden, Inc.

DATE OF ORIGIN: Unknown

INGREDIENTS: American cheese, skim milk, whey, cream, sodium citrate (improves consistency), modified whey solids, salt, sodium phosphate (improves consistency), sorbic acid (a preservative), citric acid (enhances flavor). Artificially colored.

MAKER: Borden Foods, Borden, Inc., Columbus, Ohio

SLOGAN: "If It's Borden, It's Got To Be Good!"

NOTES: Gail Borden patented a process of evaporating milk in 1856, opening the first evaporating plant in 1858. As the Borden Milk Company grew, new products were added. On the American Cheese Food package is the picture of one of America's best known company symbols, Borden's Elsie the Cow, who first appeared in cartoon form about 1936. By 1938 she began to get her own fan mail, and in 1939 the first of 15 live Elsies toured throughout the United States. Elsie appeared at World's Fairs, hotels, department stores, parties, and charity drives—later with a husband, Elmer, a daughter, Beulah, and a son, Beauregard. In the 1960s she went into limbo, but popular demand brought her back and a live Elsie began to tour again in 1971.

7UP®

DIMENSIONS: 16 oz. bottle: 10¾″ H × 2¹⁹⁄₃₂″ Diam.
12 oz. can: 4¹³⁄₁₆″ H × 2¹⁹⁄₃₂″ Diam.

PACKAGE: Bottle: Glass with metal cap. Can: Aluminum. Label designed by Lander Associates.

ORIGINATOR: C. L. Grigg

DATE OF ORIGIN: August 7, 1928

INGREDIENTS: Carbonated water, sugar and/or corn sweetener, citric acid, sodium citrate, natural lemon and lime flavors.

MAKER: The Seven-Up Company, St. Louis, Missouri

SLOGANS: "Fresh Up with 7UP"; "You Like It . . . It Likes You" (1950s and 1960s); "7UP the Uncola®" (1976); "America's Turning 7UP" (1978).

NOTES: C. L. Grigg's Howdy Company wanted to market a drink with a lemon-lime flavor. After 11 tries, "Bib-Label Lithiated Lemon-Lime Soda" was introduced—two weeks before the stock market crash in 1929. The 7UP® trademark had been registered the year before and was given to the new product, which obviously benefited from the simpler name. When scientist Joseph Priestly devised a way to put carbon dioxide into water in 1772, soda water was born. Early carbonated beverages were sealed with porcelain stoppers which, when pushed in, released the carbon dioxide in the bottle with a "pop". Hence the 1890's term "soda pop".

Onion Dip

ORIGINATOR: Unknown Californian

DATE OF ORIGIN: Circa 1950

INGREDIENTS: Commercial sour cream, packaged dried onion soup mix.

NOTES: The original southern California onion dip, influenced by nearby Mexico, was stronger and spicier than now. The recipe was printed in a California newspaper and began to spread across the country—becoming refined and modified along the way. It is now generally made by combining Lipton®onion soup mix and sour cream, and is known as California Dip. Appearing at almost every party, the dip is served with corn chips (shown), potato chips, bread sticks, or fresh raw vegetables.

Cheez-It®

DIMENSIONS: 16 oz. pkg.: 9″ H × 6¼″ W × 3″ D

PACKAGE: Recycled paperboard, printed five-color offset lithography, designed by Sangren & Murtha.

ORIGINATORS: J. L. and J. S. Loose and John A. Wiles

DATE OF ORIGIN: Early 1920s

INGREDIENTS: Enriched flour (flour, niacin, reduced iron, thiamine mononitrate, riboflavin), vegetable shortening (contains one or more of the following hydrogenated oils: soybean, cottonseed, palm, peanut, and/or coconut oil), skim milk, cheese, salt, paprika, yeast.

MAKER: Sunshine Biscuits, Inc., New York, New York

SLOGANS: "Good Any Old Time"; "America's Favorite Cheese Cracker".

NOTES: Begun in 1902, the LooseWiles Biscuit Company built the Thousand Window Bakery in 1912 in Long Island City, New York, because the owners wanted sunny working quarters instead of the dark factories common then. From this came the name Sunshine Biscuits. The building, a New York landmark, stood until the 1950s when it was then replaced by a modern bakery with band ovens the length of two football fields.

Sunshine

CHEEZ-IT
Tasty Snack Crackers

CONTAINS
100%
NATURAL CHEESE
MADE FROM SKIM MILK
NO ARTIFICIAL FLAVORS

ONE POUND SIZE

NET WT. 16 OZ. (1 LB.)
454 GRAMS

Goobers®

DIMENSIONS: 8 oz. box: 8¾″ L × 3⅝″ W × 1¾₁₆″ H

PACKAGE: SBS board, printed offset lithography, designed by Warren J. Weil.

ORIGINATOR: Joseph Blumenthal

DATE OF ORIGIN: 1924

INGREDIENTS: Peanuts, milk chocolate, sugar, soya lecithin, an emulsifier, vanillin, an artificial flavoring, salt, tapioca dextrin, resinous glaze. (Milk chocolate contains sugar, whole milk, cocoa butter, chocolate).

MAKER: Ward Candy Company, Division of Ward-Johnston, New York, New York

SLOGANS: "Chocolate Covered Treat . . . Mighty Good To Eat"© 1970; "Just Chocolate and Peanuts . . . Simply Delicious"©1979.

NOTES: Peanuts were grown by pre-Columbian Indians in South America. They were carried to Africa and then back to North America through the slave trade. Peanuts are known by many names: pinder, earthnut, groundnut, ground pea. The word "goober", which is widely used in the American South, comes from Africa, from the Bantu word for peanut, *nguba*.

Goobers won the NEWA and POPAI awards in 1979 as a leading American movie candy.

Skippy® Peanut Butter

DIMENSIONS: 18 oz. size: 5¼″ H × 3¼″ Diam.

PACKAGE: Glass, metal cap. Paper label, printed offset lithography, designed by Rosefield Packing Corp.

ORIGINATOR: Rosefield Packing Corp.

DATE OF ORIGIN: 1923

INGREDIENTS: U.S. grade no. 1 peanuts, dextrose, partially hydrogenated vegetable oil, salt, sugar.

MAKER: CPC International, Englewood Cliffs, New Jersey

SLOGAN: "It's Hard to Beat Skippy"

NOTES: Over 650,000,000 pounds of peanut butter are consumed by Americans each year, mainly in peanut butter sandwiches. There are many peanut butter recipes used in other countries, including an Ecuadorian dish of potatoes, lettuce, eggs, and peanut butter called *yapingacho*.

Baskin-Robbins Ice Cream

DIMENSIONS: 3.5 oz. scoops: approx. 2⅝″ Diam.

ORIGINATORS: Irving Robbins and Burton "Butch" Baskin

DATE OF ORIGIN: December 7, 1945

INGREDIENTS: Fresh sweet cream, whole milk, nuts, fruits, candies. Ingredients vary according to flavor.

MAKER: Baskin-Robbins Ice Cream, Glendale, California

SLOGAN: "Get That ㉛ derful Feeling"

NOTES: In 1965 there were over 1500 B-R stores in the U.S. There have been more than 400 flavors, with new ones always being planned. (See *Guiness Book of Records.*) Baskin-Robbins have their own special scoop, holding 3.5 oz. In California, Irving Robbins has an ice-cream-cone-shaped swimming pool. At night, the lighted pool is pointed out to airline passengers as a landmark.

Flavors shown: Top: Chocolate Mint, *Bottom:* Pralines 'n Cream